The Big
of Hooked Rugs
1950-1980s

Jessie A. Turbayne

Schiffer Publishing Ltd

4880 Lower Valley Road, Atglen, PA 19310 USA

Dedication

From Hallie Hall to all rug hookers:
past, present, and future

Cover rug: "Locked Leaf." Hooked by Carol Ashley Wade of Marlborough, New Hampshire. Dated 1979. Pearl McGown pattern / Old Sturbridge Village / W. Cushing and Company.

Published by Schiffer Publishing Ltd.
4880 Lower Valley Road
Atglen, PA 19310
Phone: (610) 593-1777; Fax: (610) 593-2002
E-mail: Info@schifferbooks.com

For the largest selection of fine reference books on this and related subjects, please visit our web site at
www.schifferbooks.com
We are always looking for people to write books on new and related subjects. If you have an idea for a
book please contact us at the above address.

This book may be purchased from the publisher.
Include $3.95 for shipping.
Please try your bookstore first.
You may write for a free catalog.

In Europe, Schiffer books are distributed by
Bushwood Books
6 Marksbury Ave.
Kew Gardens
Surrey TW9 4JF England
Phone: 44 (0) 20 8392-8585; Fax: 44 (0) 20 8392-9876
E-mail: info@bushwoodbooks.co.uk
Free postage in the U.K., Europe; air mail at cost.

Library of Congress Cataloging-in-Publication Data

Turbayne, Jessie A.
    The big book of hooked rugs, 1950s-1980s / by Jessie A. Turbayne.
        p. cm.
    ISBN 0-7643-2198-6 (pbk.)
    1. Rugs, Hooked—United States—History—20th century. I. Title.

NK2812.T8697 2005
746.7'4'09730904—dc22

                          2004023125

Designed by Mark David Bowyer
Type set in Windsor BT/Souvenir Lt BT

ISBN: 0-7643-2198-6
Printed in China

Contents

Acknowledgments

A special word of appreciation to Peter and Nancy Schiffer and the always helpful staff that is Schiffer Publishing, Ltd. To my editors, Donna Baker and Douglas Congdon-Martin, it has been a pleasure working with you.

Thank you to Ramona Maddox of Chattanooga, Tennessee, who years ago strongly suggested that I really should meet this extraordinary rug hooking teacher in New Hampshire named Hallie Hall.

Kudos to Judy Yasi for patiently and successfully guiding this technologically challenged author through the corridors of computer hell and always doing so with a smile.

Thank you, Jeanie Crockett, for your sense of humor and unfaltering literary skills.

To Annie Spring, who never fails to amaze me with her encyclopedia-like knowledge of rug hooking. Thank you for always answering my endless stream of questions in such a gracious and informative manner.

A very sincere word of gratitude for the late Hallie Hall, who had the insight to document such an important era in the rug hooking world. Thank you for trusting me to tell the story and show the rugs that you so dearly loved.

Kind acknowledgment to Marie Azzaro, Jeanne Benjamin, Molly Cox, Sandy Cheverie, Marion Ham, Carol Kassera, Evelyn Lawrence, Rosalie Lent, Marjorie Mello, Nancy Miner, Paul Moshimer, Rob Petta, Charlotte Price, Michael Santos, Margaret Siano, Susan Smidt, Anthony and Florence Travis, C. Allan Turbayne, James A. Turbayne, Justina Rae Two Eagle, Carol Ashley Wade, Ann Winterling, and Patricia Zeiser.

Rug Hooking–
The Pivotal Years:
1950s–1980s

Although often overlooked, the 1950s through the 1980s served as pivotal decades in the rug hooking world. Both women and men were enjoying the craft and hooking rugs in record numbers.

In the early days of the 1950s, rug hooking entrepreneurs Pearl McGown and Charlotte Stratton of Massachusetts and Louise Zeiser of Rhode Island were designing and selling thousands of preprinted patterns to eager rug hookers from the East Coast to the West Coast and everywhere in between. Patterns were the choice of rug hooking teachers and the growing numbers of students they attracted. As the demand grew, more and more new designers rushed to fill the need. Printed on burlap and available in a wide range of styles, patterns could be purchased from teachers or ordered through dozens of catalogs. While some enthusiasts opened shops, others sold their wares at rug hooking exhibits.

Most popular with rug hookers during the 1950s were floral patterns—realistic and lush and complemented by ornate scroll borders. Under the direction of skilled teachers, rug makers learned to hook life-like buds and blossoms and accompanying foliage. The rose, queen of all hooked flora, was tediously and meticulously fashioned using a 3/32-inch-wide strip of woolen fabric cut from an eight-value swatch of jewel-like colors. A stash of colorful swatches, either purchased or hand-dyed, was vital to the making of beautiful hooked rugs.

Second in popularity to floral designs were Oriental-inspired patterns. Introduced in the 1860s as "Turkish" by Maine native Edward Sands Frost, hooked Oriental rugs were back in style and all the rage from the 1950s on. With exotic names such as "Afshari," "Omar Khayyám," and "Kashmir," patterns replicated the characteristic geometric motifs of imported Orientals as well as the curving and flowing lines of Persian carpets. Hookers put forth every effort to mimic the knotted rugs they so admired.

While patterns were being promoted, individual creativity was not. It was, however, the preprinted designs and the scores of carefully trained and certified teachers that kept the tradition of rug hooking alive and thriving at a time when the craft could easily have faded away. This was the era of rug hooking teas, rug hooking bees, and donning hats and white gloves to attend the latest hooked rug exhibit.

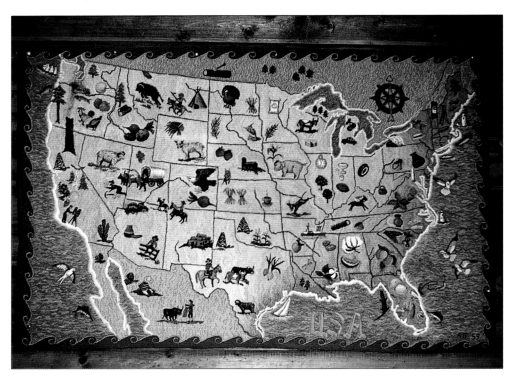

In the 1950s through the 1980s, there was a renewed interest in the tradition of rug hooking. Across the United States and Canada, women and men were hooking rugs in record number. "USA." Heirloom Rug pattern. Slide processed February 1960.

Hooking under the watchful eye of the "Godey Ladies." Charlotte Stratton pattern / Yankee Peddler. Slide processed October 1980.

By the end of the 1960s, some rug hookers grew weary of the formal rose and scroll-type patterns and sought an alternative to the often strict regimentation that many instructors faithfully followed. More and more designers were offering "something new"—a more creative approach to rug hooking. Joan Moshimer of Kennebunkport, Maine, an artist and certified McGown teacher, was instrumental in promoting this new trend in rug hooking. Others followed her lead and soon developed styles of their own.

The 1974 landmark exhibition of hooked rugs held at the Museum of American Folk Art in New York City and Joel and Kate Kopp's 1975 book *American Hooked and Sewn Rugs—Folk Art Underfoot,* which documented the exhibited rugs, introduced modern-day rug hookers to primitive imagery. Many embraced the free-spirited ideas and never looked back.

Due to the insight of the late beloved New Hampshire rug hooking artist and teacher Hallie Hall (1908–2001), we are able to view a wide sampling of the rugs that were being hooked and exhibited during the 1950s through the mid-1980s. Hallie, with permission, photographed (in the form of slides) hooked rug exhibits that took place in New England, West Virginia, and the Long Island district of New York. Also on view here are rugs that traveled from Mississippi, Alabama, Wisconsin, and Ohio, as well as other states.

In October of 1994, Hallie, having relocated to Hood River, Oregon, to be closer to family, sent me her collection of five hundred slides and permission to use them as I saw fit. We had at that time discussed the possibility of a future book. "Keep the ones you like and throw the others away." None were tossed. With Hallie's whole-hearted approval I have put them all together in this album, which documents the pivotal years of rug hooking—the 1950s through the mid-1980s.

Interlocking gold rings, a hooked tribute to wedded bliss. Slide processed September 1980.

Disclaimer

Because of her enthusiasm to capture photographically all that was on display, little or no information was recorded about the rugs, their makers, and the locations or dates of the exhibits. But we will forgive Hallie, for she did indeed visually document a very important era in rug hooking.

I truly regret not being able to identify all the makers of all the rugs. Hallie would want to give credit to the hooking artists, many of whom were her students, but names, unfortunately, were not often recorded.

Whenever possible, I have noted the date the slides were processed. Knowing Hallie as I did, the time between the actual taking of the slides and the processing was brief.

Trying to trace the pattern makers of these illustrated rugs was at times difficult. Over the years, small businesses frequently changed hands and those transaction dates are not always available. Designs and patterns traveled near and far. Whenever possible, I have included the name of the pattern maker at the time the rug was hooked and/or photographed, as well as the subsequent and current owners of the copyright to that pattern. For example, the caption under a 1958 floral design might read: Pearl McGown pattern / Old Sturbridge Village / W. Cushing and Company.

Rug hookers love to work with color. "Bottles" offered the challenge of hooking the reflecting light that radiates from antique glass. Pearl McGown pattern / Old Sturbridge Village / W. Cushing and Company.

Hooked Rug Pattern Makers—A Time Line

Ralph Burnham, "Hooked Rug Magnate" of the early 1900s, bought, sold, repaired, and reproduced thousands of rugs from his Ipswich, Massachusetts, Antique Trading Post. To preserve the antique rug designs that he fancied, Burnham made paper tracings of many of the rugs that passed through his shop. In 1922, he started producing burlap rug patterns for sale. Burnham died in 1938 and his wife, Nellie, continued the business until 1957. Eventually **Ruth Hall**, a New Hampshire rug hooking teacher and designer, purchased the patterns. Mrs. Hall in turn sold the designs to **W. Cushing and Company** of Kennebunkport, Maine, which now reprints many of Burnham's favorites.

Lib Callaway Patterns of New Canaan, Connecticut, established in the late-1970s, featured primitive folk art designs. The Callaway patterns were sold to **Margaret Siano** in 1995 and are available through the **Hook Nook** in Flemington, New Jersey.

DiFranza Designs has been owned and operated by Steve and Happy DiFranza of Reading, Massachusetts, since 1968.

Edana Designs was started by Edith Dana of Darien, Connecticut. She was a student of Caroline Saunders, a popular Massachusetts rug hooking teacher in the 1930s and 1940s. The Edana Designs were sold to Marion Ham–**Quail Hill Designs** of Clark, New Jersey, in 1981. Quail Hill Designs continues under the ownership of Marion Ham and is now located in Brunswick, Maine.

Jane McGown Flynn of Sterling, Massachusetts, granddaughter of Pearl McGown, designed hooked rug patterns and offered them through her 1980 catalog *Designs to Dream On.* In 1998, the Flynn patterns were sold to **The House of Price, Inc.–Charco Patterns,** which is currently owned and operated by Charlotte Price and located in Mars, Pennsylvania.

Edward Sands Frost (1843–1894) of Maine was the first widely known commercial maker of hooked rug patterns. In 1876, due to poor health, Frost sold his pattern business to James A. Strout, mayor of Biddeford, Maine, who continued to do business under the name of E. S. Frost & Company. During this time, several small companies began to print and distribute rug patterns, many copying Frost's original compositions, which were never copyrighted. Ebenezer Ross of Toledo, Ohio, inventor of an "automated" punch hook, published in 1891 a catalog of rug patterns, the majority being variations of Frost's handiwork. In 1900, Mayor Strout sold

Frost's metal stencils to Henry F. Whiting, a belt manufacturer, of Lowell, Massachusetts. Fortunately, the hundreds of stencils that Frost fashioned and used to print his designs were saved from being sold as scrap metal when rug hooking teacher and designer **Charlotte Stratton**, of Vermont, purchased them from the Whiting family in 1936. Mrs. Stratton reproduced and sold Frost patterns until her retirement from active teaching in 1958. That year, the stencils were obtained by **Greenfield Village–Henry Ford Museum** in Dearborn, Michigan, which used them in their crafts program until about 1980. In 2003, the **Maine State Museum** in Augusta acquired the majority of the stencils that Frost made from the Henry Ford Museum. Over the years, many pattern makers, including **Pearl McGown** and **W. Cushing and Company**, have offered variations of the Frost designs.

Heirloom Rugs was started by Louise Zeiser of Providence, Rhode Island, in the 1940s. Prior to establishing her own business, Mrs. Zeiser designed exclusively for Caroline Saunders, a popular Massachusetts rug hooking teacher in the 1930s and 1940s. Heirloom and **Hookraft** patterns, designed by Mrs. Zeiser, were available through the Heirloom catalog, as were the designs of **Margaret Mackenzie**, creator of the **Skaket** line. In later years, ownership was transferred to Louise's son Robert, of Rumford, Rhode Island, who continued to print and sell the popular Heirloom line. In the 1990s, the Heirloom patterns were sold to Connecticut buyers.

Karlkraft Studio, owned by Helen Carlson and most likely established in the 1940s, moved from Illinois to Maine to New Hampshire. The business was sold once before **Braid-Aid**, a retail and catalog company specializing in braiding and hooking supplies, located in Pembroke, Massachu-

When it comes to rug hooking, variety is the spice of life. Slide processed September 1980.

setts, bought the line of Karlkraft patterns in the 1980s. In 2004, the Karlkraft patterns were sold to a buyer in Texas.

Margaret Hunt Masters, of Wisconsin, Ohio, and Missouri, was a popular rug hooking teacher and designer during the 1940s and 1950s. Her patterns were sold to **Prairie Craft House**. Prairie Craft House is owned and operated by Carol Kassera of Aledo, Texas.

Pearl McGown (1892–1983), the West Boylston, Massachusetts-based grande dame of rug hooking from the 1930s through the 1960s, authored four books, trained hundreds of rug hooking teachers, and throughout her career maintained a quota of releasing a dozen new patterns per month. In 1970, the rights to the McGown designs, all aspects of the business, and many of the rugs from Rose Cottage, her home and studio, were sold to **Old Sturbridge Village** of Sturbridge, Massachusetts. In the early 1980s, **W. Cushing and Company** of Kennebunkport, Maine, purchased the rights to the Pearl McGown patterns and currently offers them under the Old Sturbridge Village (OSV) name.

Joan Moshimer (1923–2000), a New Zealand born artist brought to the United States by her husband, Robert, after World War II, was largely responsible during the 1970s, and faithfully thereafter, for renewing an interest in rug hooking. In 1968, Joan opened the doors to her Kennebunkport, Maine, studio and began doing business under the name of **W. Cushing and Company**. In addition to designing her own patterns, she authored two books and for eighteen years wrote and edited *Rug Hooker News and Views,* a popular magazine that attracted an international audience. W. Cushing and Company is now managed by the Moshimers' son, Paul.

New Earth Designs was started by Pamela Ashworth Jones of Ipswich, Massachusetts, in 1970, sold to the Rugar family of New York in 1983, and has been owned and operated by Jeanne Benjamin of Brookfield, Massachusetts, since 1992.

Charlotte Stratton established Yankee Peddler Studio in Montpelier, Vermont, in the 1930s and operated it through 1950. There she taught rug hooking, trained teachers, gave instructions in dyeing, and designed and sold patterns. In 1936, Mrs. Stratton added the Edward Sands Frost designs to her catalog. Around 1950, Mrs. Stratton moved to Greenfield, Massachusetts, and continued doing business as The Old New England Hooked Rug Craft Studio. Upon her retirement from active teaching in 1958, the Frost patterns were turned over to Greenfield Village–Henry Ford Museum in Dearborn, Michigan. All other Charlotte Stratton designs went to **Ruth Davis** in Trumbull, Connecticut. In 1979, Ruth Davis sold the patterns to Marie Azzaro of Killingworth, Connecticut, who currently sells rug hooking supplies under the name of **Yankee Peddler**.

Setting Up the Show

A small army of volunteers was needed to hang a hooked rug exhibit. During the 1950s and into the 1980s, church and town halls, school and college cafeterias, libraries, and civic centers, available for little or no money, were used by rug hooking groups eager to show off their handiwork. Those groups offering shows of two hundred or more rugs often pooled their funds and rented larger accommodations. Slide processed September 1980.

Once the hooked rugs arrived at the exhibit area they were sorted into categories such as floral, geometric, Oriental, etc. Each piece was given a label identifying the person who hooked the rug and often where they lived, the designer or pattern maker, and the name of the rug hooker's teacher. At times, the hooked pieces were assigned numbers only. An accompanying flyer or catalog listing the numbered rugs and containing pertinent information was given to those who came to view the display.

Each rug received special treatment and was carefully hung. Slide processed November 1960.

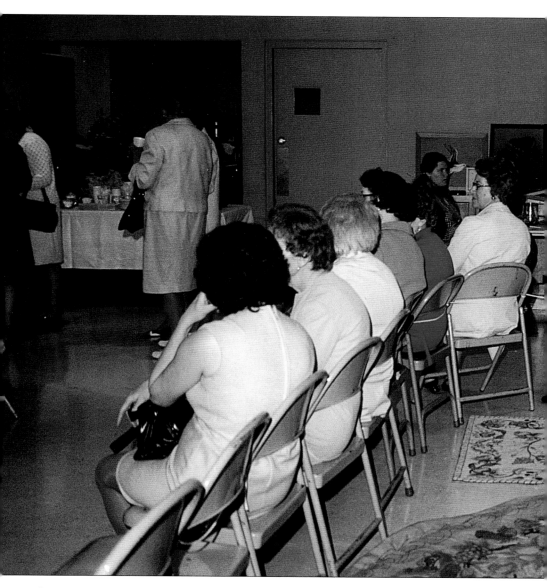

Classes and/or lectures were often held during the exhibits. Rug hookers were and still are always eager to learn more about their favorite craft. Slide processed June 1972.

If the weather permitted, rug makers sometimes opted to display their hooked works out of doors. Slide processed June 1972.

Natural light is best for viewing hand-hooked pieces. Slide processed June 1972.

Floral Designs— Rectangular Rugs

"Challenge." Touches of light grace both the floral centerpiece and complementary scroll border. Pearl McGown pattern / Old Sturbridge Village / W. Cushing and Company. Slide processed March 1961.

A hooked garden center brightens subdued scrolls and background.

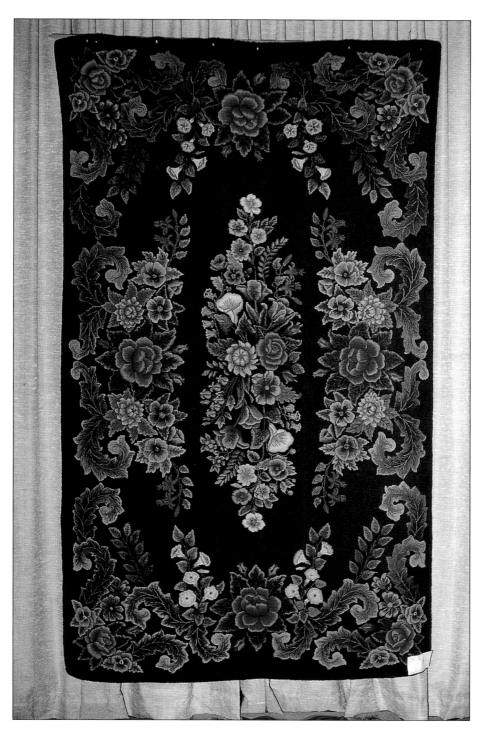

Lush roses enhance a medley of blossoms. Karlkraft pattern / Braid-Aid. Slide processed December 1963.

Red, white, and blue flowers, perhaps fashioned by a patriotic rug hooker, are framed by two ornate scroll borders.

Poinsettias, pinecones, and holly add a note of cheer to a rug with winter theme. Initialed GT. Dated [19]62. Slide processed July 1963.

"Persian Paradise." Center floral arrangement and corner sprays are vibrant against a rich dark background. Pearl McGown pattern / Old Sturbridge Village / W. Cushing and Company.

"Ruby." A two-toned background complements the flowers that rest upon it. Pearl McGown pattern / Old Sturbridge Village / W. Cushing and Company. Slide processed March 1961.

A flowery show. Hooked gardens on display.

Opposite page:
Soft and subtle "Gretchen." Use of a
limited palette makes for a pleasing rug.
Pearl McGown pattern / Old Sturbridge
Village / W. Cushing and Company.
Slide processed December 1963.

Stylized flowers spring forth and are enhanced by contrasting backgrounds. Slide processed October 1967.

Lush and radiant. "Romantique." Pearl McGown pattern / Old Sturbridge Village / W. Cushing and Company. Slide processed May 1973.

Shades of amethyst prevail. Close-up of "Romantique." Pearl McGown pattern / Old Sturbridge Village / W. Cushing and Company. Slide processed May 1973.

Leaves, a delicate shade of green, rest upon curlicue scrolls. Close-up of "Romantique." Pearl McGown pattern / Old Sturbridge Village / W. Cushing and Company. Slide processed May 1973.

A harmonious blend of subtle shades. Close-up of "Romantique." Pearl McGown pattern / Old Sturbridge Village / W. Cushing and Company. Slide processed May 1973.

A prize-winning "Calla Lily Wreath," surrounded by heavily fruited grape vines. Pearl McGown pattern / Old Sturbridge Village / W. Cushing and Company. Slide processed November 1960.

Another version of "Calla Lily Wreath." Pearl McGown pattern / Old Sturbridge Village / W. Cushing and Company. Slide processed March 1961.

"Velvet Flowers." Summer blossoms by the dozen. Heirloom Rug pattern.

"Velvet Flowers" underfoot. Pleasing to the eye and soft to the touch. Hooked by Hazel Dykes. Heirloom Rug pattern. Slide processed September 1961.

Surrounded by a vivid blue scroll, buds and blossoms by the score cling to an interior oval support.

"First and Second Fiddle." The colors used to fashion the central bouquet brighten the inner and outer borders. Pearl McGown pattern / Old Sturbridge Village / W. Cushing and Company. Slide processed September 1980.

Hooked flowers rest upon Mother Nature's carpet of green.

Shades of lavender, combined with pussy willow branches, jonquils, and assorted floral sprays, tell of bright spring days. "Memoria." Pearl McGown pattern / Old Sturbridge Village / W. Cushing and Company. Slide processed March 1966.

Curlicue scrolls accentuate a colorful floral arrangement. "Duke of Marlborough."
Pearl McGown pattern / Old Sturbridge Village / W. Cushing and Company.

Opposite page:
An angular leaf-like border frames a floral spray of roses and delphiniums.

Sporting a different look. The aforementioned rose and delphinium pattern hooked with a golden field.

"Lilac Time." Swags of stylized leaves encase roses, tulips, and lilac. Heirloom Rug pattern.

Swirling scrolls, hooked from a tweedy fabric, protect a central corsage.

A quaint nosegay complemented by a trio of pansies.

Visually striking; a rug sure to be the focal point of any room.

"Lush" tulips and morning glories take center stage. Pearl McGown pattern / Old Sturbridge Village / W. Cushing and Company.

"It's a Cinch." A neutral background highlights roses, pansies, iris, and posies. The shades of yellow and green used in the leaves and flowers are repeated in the border design. Pearl McGown pattern / Old Sturbridge Village / W. Cushing and Company. Slide processed June 1960.

"The Patrician" unites sharp picket fence and saw-toothed borders with an array of fragile summer flowers. Pearl McGown pattern / Old Sturbridge Village / W. Cushing and Company. Slide processed June 1961.

Twisting and turning scrolls of a delicate nature rest upon a blue field and protect the center bouquet. Initialed GRT. Dated [19]59. Slide processed June 1960.

Tribute is paid to one's English, Scottish, and Irish heritage. Roses and thistles join shamrocks. Slide processed September 1961.

Unrestrained scrolls tame twin floral sprays. Initialed MB. Dated [19]59. Slide processed April 1959.

Floral sprays, almost unnoticed in the aforementioned rug, are brought to life when placed against somber scrolls and a dark background. Slide processed June 1960.

On display and waiting to be admired. Slide processed December 1963.

The colors used to hook buds, blossoms, and leaves are also found in this rug's lively scroll border. Pearl McGown pattern / Old Sturbridge Village / W. Cushing and Company. Slide processed December 1963.

Another successful blending of color. The same pattern as the aforementioned rug, but executed in a different manner. Hooked by Peg (Margaret) Draper in 1957. Pearl McGown pattern / Old Sturbridge Village / W. Cushing and Company. Slide processed February 1958.

"Perfume Box" brings together carnations, hibiscus, and phlox. A lattice-like fence contains the central floral motifs. Pearl McGown pattern / Old Sturbridge Village / W. Cushing and Company.

A royal rug indeed. "Queen's Desire." Hooked by Jane Lett. Pearl McGown pattern / Old Sturbridge Village / W. Cushing and Company.

"Roumanian Convent " wears a ribbon of merit. Heirloom Rug pattern.

At an exhibit there were hooked rugs everywhere you looked. Slide processed September 1980.

"Amber Grain" forms the border around an abundant harvest of flowers. Heirloom Rug pattern. Slide processed June 1960.

All that is needed to complete this cheerful rug is to sew the binding in place. "Nasturtiums." Pearl McGown pattern / Old Sturbridge Village / W. Cushing and Company.

Half-round floral wreath, complete with butterfly, rests upon a rectangular neutral field.

A garden of "Iris" blow in an imaginary wind. Heirloom Rug pattern.

"Hallelujah." This rug of roses was worthy of a blue ribbon. Heirloom Rug pattern.

No sitting on this bench. Every available space was used to display rugs during an exhibit. Woodland pine boughs and pinecones rest beside garden buds and blossoms. Slide processed September 1980.

Wildfowl take cover in forest flora and fauna. Slide processed October 1961.

A closer look at the aforementioned wildfowl hooked rug.

"Old New England." An Heirloom Rug pattern that our photographer Hallie Hall noted was their largest. 10' x 15'. Slide processed March 1966.

Opposite page:
Designed and hooked
by Celia Rush, this
elegant Aubusson-style
salute to roses dons a
blue ribbon.

Floral Sprays

Branches of magnolia are set against a dusty rose background. "Southern Belle." Note the ribbon of merit. Pearl McGown pattern / Old Sturbridge Village / W. Cushing and Company. Slide processed November 1960.

A dark brown field is the backdrop for clusters of "Dogwood" flowers.
Hooked by Gladys Fountain. Pearl McGown pattern / Old Sturbridge
Village / W. Cushing and Company. Slide processed October 1962.

A painting on velvet? No. It's a hooked still life of roses. Slide processed November 1958.

Cut flowers adorned by snail and butterfly. "P-105." Pearl McGown pattern / Old Sturbridge Village / W. Cushing and Company.

An elegant S-shaped garland hooked from many shades of one color. Slide processed November 1958.

Roses and tulips added a touch of color to an otherwise plain interior.

A twisted rope border surrounds bouquets of tulips, pansies, and dogwood. "Venus."
Pearl McGown pattern / Old Sturbridge Village / W. Cushing and Company.

Flowery stems. Roses, buds, and leaves twist and turn.

Floral Designs—Ovals

Mastering the art of hooking a rose was of utmost importance to all rug makers.
Colors not found in nature were used to create life-like roses, lilies, and foliage.

A harmonious combination of floral center and "Stag Horn Scroll." Initialed MDM. Dated [19]72. Pearl McGown pattern / Old Sturbridge Village / W. Cushing and Company. Slide processed June 1973.

A bountiful bouquet of morning glories takes center stage. Slide processed April 1964.

Bright and cheerful; an elongated wreath of pansies delights one and all. Slide processed July 1963.

Interlocking fronds of stylized leaves form a decorative band around a botanical master-piece. Initialed LG. Dated [19]79.

A diminutive wreath of leaves separates an inner floral cluster from an outer floral border.

"Staffordshire Oval." A band of clover encompasses a garden of both realistic and fanciful flowers. Hooked in 1959. Pearl McGown pattern / Old Sturbridge Village / W. Cushing and Company. Slide processed June 1959.

On display in the hooked rug flower garden is another version of "Staffordshire Oval." Pearl McGown pattern / Old Sturbridge Village / W. Cushing and Company. Slide processed November 1981.

In the words of our photographer Hallie Hall, "My first large rug. Long Island. 8' x 10'." Edward Sands Frost pattern / Charlotte Stratton / Greenfield Village–Henry Ford Museum / Maine State Museum.

Shades of red and green predominate. Decorative borders encircle a quartet of roses.

Described as a "fat" oval, "The Aristocrat" (72" x 96") was hooked by Jane Lett of New York. Teacher Hallie Hall. This beautiful rug of gold, bronze, and mummy browns was pictured in Pearl McGown's 1966 book *The Lore and Lure of Hooked Rugs*. Pearl McGown pattern / Old Sturbridge Village / W. Cushing and Company.

Close-up of Jane Lett's "Aristocrat." Pearl McGown pattern / Old Sturbridge Village / W. Cushing and Company.

Having enough space to properly display hooked rugs at an exhibit was always a problem.

Opposite page:
Hooked "Geraniums" are
draped above potted
geraniums. Margaret
Mackenzie–Skaket /
Heirloom Rug pattern. Slide
processed September 1980.

Floral Designs—Round

Informal yet refreshing. Hooked daisies form a simple wreath. Slide processed November 1964.

Elaborate and resplendent scrolls circle roses, chrysanthemums, tulips, and foxglove stems. Ferns were added to the floral foliage. "Gainsborough." Pearl McGown pattern / Old Sturbridge Village / W. Cushing and Company.

Opposite page, top:
"Gainsborough." Hooked
by Helen Connelly of North
Port, Long Island, New
York. Jewel-like scrolls
enhance the floral center-
piece. Pearl McGown
pattern / Old Sturbridge
Village / W. Cushing and
Company. Slide processed
November 1970.

Roses and pansies steal the show.

Opposite page, bottom:
A closer look at Helen
Connelly's "Gainsborough."
Pearl McGown pattern / Old
Sturbridge Village / W.
Cushing and Company. Slide
processed November 1970.

Fuchsias and geraniums spring forth from a dainty wicker basket.

Opposite page:
"Sandwich Cup Plate"
replicates a popular pattern
used by one of the several
glass companies located in
Sandwich, Massachusetts,
that produced wares
between 1825 and 1922.
Margaret Mackenzie–Skaket /
Heirloom Rug pattern.

C-shaped scrolls complement a glorious centerpiece. Slide processed April 1975.

Exhibit visitors were delighted to find a wide variety of hooked rugs. Slide processed September 1980.

On display were hooked rugs of all shapes and sizes. Slide processed September 1980.

Opposite page:
The start of a floral, foliage, and fruit sampler. Such studies were used to train and certify McGown rug hooking teachers. Pearl McGown patterns / Old Sturbridge Village / W. Cushing and Company.

Floral Grid

Fifteen flowers compose the floral sampler that is a "Garden's Gift." Pearl McGown pattern / Old Sturbridge Village / W. Cushing and Company. Slide processed April 1966.

"Garden's Gift" with a light background takes on a different look. Pearl McGown pattern / Old Sturbridge Village / W. Cushing and Company.

Roses in various stages of bloom rest within a lattice-work grid. Hooked by Ann Tatuni. Slide processed June 1960.

Opposite page:
A trio of blossoms
fills every other row
of stylized diamonds.
Slide processed
September 1980.

"Kent Hit or Miss" was most likely named for a rug in the collection of hooked rug collector, enthusiast, and author William Winthrop Kent (1860–1955). Hooked by Alice Kelley in 1957. Charlotte Stratton pattern / Ruth Davis / Yankee Peddler.

Floral nosegays, each slightly different, form a cheerful pattern underfoot.

Stylized leaves and berries form a repeat tile-like pattern. Slide processed June 1960.

This rug, comprised of ornamental panels, was inspired by the raised enamel decorations known as "Cloisonnes." Hooked by Alice Kelley in 1957. Margaret Mackenzie–Skaket / Heirloom Rug pattern. Slide processed in February 1958.

"Winter Bloom" is ready to warm a cold, dreary day. Hooked in 1954. Pearl McGown pattern / Old Sturbridge Village / W. Cushing and Company.

Opposite page:
A pair of flowery bands, each featuring a central "Dahlia." Pearl McGown pattern / Old Sturbridge Village / W. Cushing and Company.

Floral Study

"Royalty." A traditional floral still life complete with ornate leafy border scroll. Pearl McGown pattern / Old Sturbridge Village / W. Cushing and Company. Slide processed September 1972.

Opposite page:
Nature's uncultivated gifts. "Wild Flower Trellis." Joan Moshimer design–W. Cushing and Company. Slide processed September 1980.

"French Bouquet." A floral study similar to the aforementioned "Royalty" but minus the ornate border. Pearl McGown pattern / Old Sturbridge Village / W. Cushing and Company.

"1825." Adapted from an antique rug. Three blue birds swoop down on fancy and free flowers. Hooked by Anna Roberts. Dated 1979. Edana (Edith Dana) pattern / Quail Hill Designs. Slide processed September 1980.

"Birds of Paradise." An inviting welcome mat of vase, blossoms, heart, twin birds, and flowing ribbon banner. Pearl McGown pattern / Old Sturbridge Village / W. Cushing and Company. Slide processed August 1971.

A bowl of pansies for your thoughts. Hooked by Alice Kelley. Slide processed May 1973.

Hibiscus study framed and ready to hang. Hooked in 1967. Slide processed in October 1967.

Waiting for the nod of approval; a trio of floral samplers. Slide processed September 1980.

Another sampler featuring the queen of all flowers, the rose.

Blooms, buds, and berries form a diminutive study. Slide processed August 1972.

Bursting blossoms of a fanciful nature. Slide processed August 1971.

Leaves, Needles,
and Mushrooms

A "Maze Border" surrounds simplified rectangles of leaves and berries. The original design included clusters of grapes. Pearl McGown pattern / Old Sturbridge Village / W. Cushing and Company. Slide processed March 1966.

Opposite page:
Assorted leaves, pine needles, and pinecones join together in this award-winning runner. Exhibited at the 1957 Women's International Exposition, New York City, New York. Pearl McGown pattern / Old Sturbridge Village / W. Cushing and Company.

An abundance of fern-like leaves, contained by leafy outer scrolls, covers a neutral field. Hooked by Mrs. Buenda. Exhibited at the Women's International Exposition in New York City, New York. Year unknown. Margaret Mackenzie–Skaket / Heirloom Rug pattern.

Similar in style to the designs of Nova Scotia's Garrett's Bluenose rug hooking patterns. Identified by our photographer Hallie Hall as "New Hampshire Antique Leaf." Hooked by Elizabeth Woodward in 1954.

"Seashore." Seashells, pinecones, seaweed, and sea grapes gathered on the shores of Florida's Fort Lauderdale inspired this unusual motif. Information from Pearl McGown's 1966 book *The Lore and Lure of Hooked Rugs*. Pearl McGown pattern / Old Sturbridge Village / W. Cushing and Company. Slide processed June 1960.

Birds lighting on leafy branches decorate a set of four pillows. Slide processed September 1980.

No aspect of nature was left unhooked. A small and charming study of mushrooms complete with tiny elf. Pearl McGown pattern / Old Sturbridge Village / W. Cushing and Company. Slide processed October 1967.

Opposite page:
Rug hooker's fungi fantasy. A mushroom panel rests beside a draped "Fairy's Cushions." Pearl McGown pattern / Old Sturbridge Village / W. Cushing and Company. Slide processed September 1980.

Floral Folk Art

A glowing and glorious adaptation of an antique rug. "Chilcott Double Cornucopia." Hooked by Mildred Schreabe in 1957. Pearl McGown pattern / Old Sturbridge Village / W. Cushing and Company.

Folk art-style flowers spring forth from a simple compote. Grapevines encompass the study forming a three-quarters frame. "Aunt Mag." Margaret Mackenzie–Skaket / Heirloom Rug pattern.

Alice Beatty, one of New Jersey's rug hooking grande dames, fashioned "The Wedding Rug" after its antique counterpart. Ruth Hall pattern / W. Cushing and Company. Slide processed November 1958.

Eight bunches of lollipop-like flowers create a pleasing pattern. Slide processed October 1965.

"Sailcloth Primitive." A center detail dated 1983. Reflecting the style and design of a much older rug. Heirloom Rug pattern.

A hooked rug reminiscent of Pennsylvania Dutch designs and traditional quilt patterns. Initialed AHI. Dated 1961. Karlkraft pattern / Braid-Aid. Slide processed November 1962.

Another rug hooker's interpretation of the aforementioned pattern. Karlkraft pattern / Braid-Aid. Slide processed February 1965.

Antique benches were used for displaying primitive-style hooked rugs. "Tate House Primitive" is seen in the foreground. Ralph Burnham pattern / Ruth Hall / W. Cushing and Company. Slide processed September 1980.

"Old Nutfield" (in the foreground) offers subdued shades against a dark background. Ralph Burnham pattern / Ruth Hall / W. Cushing and Company. Slide processed September 1980.

Tree of Life

"Lucetta's Tree of Life," full of fanciful details, was a very popular pattern to hook. Pearl McGown pattern / Old Sturbridge Village / W. Cushing and Company. Slide processed June 1960.

Another interpretation of "Lucetta's Tree of Life." Pearl McGown pattern /
Old Sturbridge Village / W. Cushing and Company. Slide processed
August 1969.

Yet another "Lucetta's Tree of Life." Pearl McGown pattern / Old Sturbridge Village / W. Cushing and Company. Slide processed September 1969.

"Lucetta's Tree of Life" hosting a dark background. Pearl McGown pattern / Old Sturbridge Village / W. Cushing and Company. Slide processed February 1980.

"Lucetta's Tree of Life" complete with two eye-catching doves. Pearl McGown pattern / Old Sturbridge Village / W. Cushing and Company. Slide processed November 1981.

This prize-winning "Tree of Life" was exhibited at the 1957 International Women's Exposition in New York City, New York. Charlotte Stratton pattern / Ruth Davis / Yankee Peddler.

A trio of birds. "Tree of Life." Initialed RH. Dated 1960. Slide processed October 1961.

Imaginary "Birds in a Tree." Margaret Mackenzie–Skaket / Heirloom Rug pattern. Slide processed June 1960.

"Birds in a Tree" with a dark background. Margaret Mackenzie–Skaket / Heirloom Rug pattern.

Crewel Designs

Crewel embroidery was developed in the seventeenth century during the reign of Queen Elizabeth I. Twentieth-century rug hookers and pattern makers embraced the fanciful motifs and produced a record number of crewel-inspired rugs. Pearl McGown first introduced these popular designs into her collection of hooked rug patterns in 1957. "Queen Mary," an exceptional example of a crewel-inspired hooked rug, is guarded by mythical unicorns. "The Unicorn" (on the right) was adapted from the famous tapestry in The Cloisters (Metropolitan Museum of Art, New York City, New York). Pearl McGown patterns / Old Sturbridge Village / W. Cushing and Company. Slide processed September 1980.

Another version of "Queen Mary." Pearl McGown pattern / Old Sturbridge Village / W. Cushing and Company. Slide processed June 1960.

A nearly complete "Queen Mary." Pearl McGown pattern / Old Sturbridge Village / W. Cushing and Company. Slide processed October 1961.

"Inheritance" is "Queen Mary" minus its ornate outer border.
Pearl McGown pattern / Old Sturbridge Village / W. Cushing and
Company. Slide processed March 1961.

Prize-winning "Duke of Devonshire." Pearl McGown pattern / Old Sturbridge Village / W. Cushing and Company. Slide processed November 1960.

Opposite page:
"Duke of Devonshire" features branches that cross and re-cross, giving life to a variety of imaginary flora. Pearl McGown pattern / Old Sturbridge Village / W. Cushing and Company. Slide processed April 1965.

Yet another "Duke of Devonshire." Pearl McGown pattern / Old Sturbridge Village / W. Cushing and Company. Slide processed October 1961.

Twin crewel sprays, grand and glorious. Slide processed February 1980.

A zigzagged border contains a matched pair of heavily laden crewel-inspired trees.
"Kensington." Complete with maker's name. Dated 1964. Pearl McGown pattern / Old
Sturbridge Village / W. Cushing and Company. Slide processed November 1964.

Crewel stems emerge from all four corners. Hooked by Peg Draper. Slide processed
October 1961.

"Tree of Life" hooked crewel panel. A central stalk bends under the weight of its fanciful vegetation. Slide processed June 1973.

Our photographer Hallie Hall identifies this pattern as "Pearl McGown's first 'Crewel' design." Pearl McGown pattern / Old Sturbridge Village / W. Cushing and Company. Slide processed September 1964.

A continuous elliptical border frames "Cape Shore Crewel." Joan Moshimer design–W. Cushing and Company. Slide processed September 1980.

Grace Kimball hooked "Cape Shore Crewel" without its looped motif. Joan Moshimer design–W. Cushing and Company. Slide processed September 1980.

Framed and ready to complement a traditional décor. Slide processed April 1969.

Sturdy stalks spurt forth imaginary flowers. Slide processed June 1960.

Twisting and turning vines radiate from a central floral medallion. Slide processed
October 1980.

Entwined flora and foliage. A reverse-image crewel pattern. Slide processed October 1961.

The same pattern as the aforementioned but of a lighter palette. Slide processed July 1963.

Yet another interpretation of a favorite crewel pattern. Slide processed October 1965.

Serpentine vines form "Crewel Antique." Margaret Mackenzie–Skaket / Heirloom Rug
pattern. Slide processed April 1964.

Close-up of another version of "Crewel Antique." Margaret Mackenzie–Skaket / Heirloom Rug pattern. Slide processed May 1973.

A simple crewel design in the works. Slide processed July 1979.

Hooked studies. "Crewel Branch," an original crewel design, rests beside "Ravar Center." Pearl McGown pattern / Old Sturbridge Village / W. Cushing and Company. Slide processed September 1980.

Innovative display. Small framed pieces sit on a baseboard heating unit and share space with a draped crewel-inspired rug. Slide processed June 1972.

Close-up of "Pastoral Scene." Edana (Edith Dana) pattern / Quail Hill Designs. Slide processed April 1971.

Rosemaling

Rosemaling, a Scandinavian style of painting found on walls, furniture, and wooden dinnerware, inspired both rug hookers and pattern makers. Slide processed April 1980.

A sturdy container supports a stylized stalk. Rosemaling hooked panel. "P-106." Pearl McGown pattern / Old Sturbridge Village / W. Cushing and Company. Slide processed October 1967.

A hooked rosemaling project off to a good start.

Fruits and Vegetables

The fruits and vegetables that are "Your Vitamins." Charlotte Stratton pattern / Ruth Davis / Yankee Peddler. Slide processed July 1961.

Hooked "Apples" and "Grapes" ready to grace your dining room chairs. Joan Moshimer designs–W. Cushing and Company. Slide processed February 1977.

More decorative chair pads. "Pears" and "Cherries." Joan Moshimer designs–W. Cushing and Company. Slide processed February 1977.

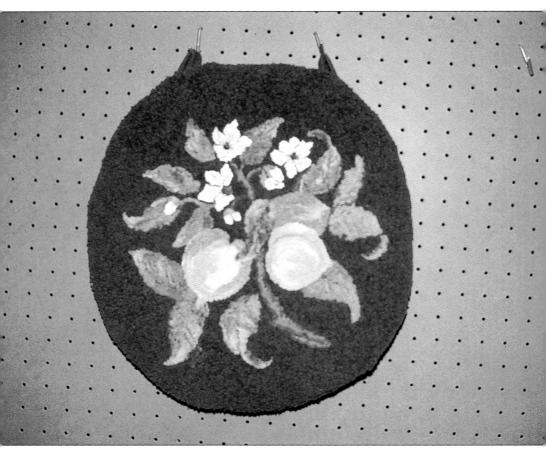

A trio of "Peaches" complete with flowers and foliage. Joan Moshimer design–W. Cushing and Company. Slide processed February 1977.

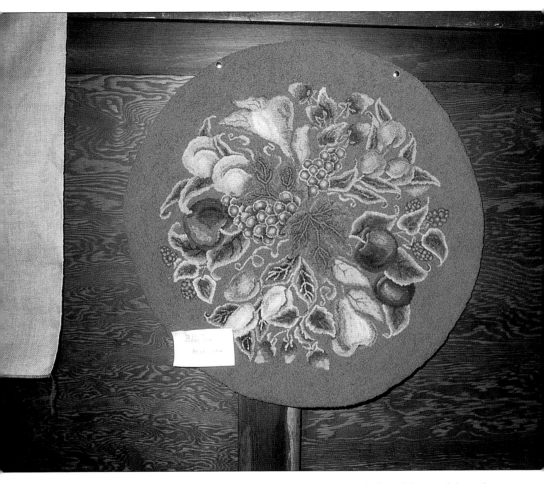

"Bounty" could be used either on a chair or as a decorative touch for table or sideboard. Pearl McGown pattern / Old Sturbridge Village / W. Cushing and Company.

A prize-winning "Bounty" of a different color scheme. Pearl McGown pattern / Old Sturbridge Village / W. Cushing and Company. Slide processed November 1960.

Opposite page:
A set of six chair pads, each of a different fruit design. Slide processed September 1980.

"Fairfax" and "Ripe Cherries" chair pads were hooked by Elsie Kraus in 1955. Heirloom Rug pattern.

"Fruit Panel(s)," by the pair, hooked and framed. Pearl McGown pattern / Old Sturbridge Village / W. Cushing and Company. Slide processed October 1967.

Same patterns as the aforementioned "Fruit Panel." Pearl McGown pattern / Old
Sturbridge Village / W. Cushing and Company. Slide processed October 1987.

Opposite page:
A heavily laden banner of fruit.
"Enough." Hooked by our
photographer Hallie Hall. Dated
1972. Pearl McGown pattern / Old
Sturbridge Village / W. Cushing
and Company. Slide processed
April 1975.

Rug hookers just couldn't get "Enough" fruit. Pearl
McGown pattern / Old Sturbridge Village / W. Cushing
and Company. Slide processed 1971.

"Enough" and "Tulips and Lilac" share a space with "Fruit Bowl Primitive." Pearl
McGown patterns / Old Sturbridge Village / W. Cushing and Company. Joan Moshimer
design–W. Cushing and Company. Slide processed September 1980.

A rosemaling panel separates a trio of "Fruit Bell Pull(s)." Rarely used for their intended purpose, hooked bell pulls were strictly decorative. Pearl McGown pattern / Old Sturbridge Village / W. Cushing and Company. Slide processed October 1967.

"Garden Orchard and Vine." A still life created with finely cut woolen fabric strips on a burlap canvas. Paintings and prints inspired both rug hookers and pattern makers. Edana (Edith Dana) pattern / Quail Hill Designs. Slide processed October 1965.

The aforementioned "Garden Orchard and Vine" was admired at several rug exhibits. Edana (Edith Dana) pattern / Quail Hill Designs. Slide processed March 1966.

Close-up of "Garden Orchard and Vine." Edana (Edith Dana) pattern / Quail Hill
Designs. Slide processed March 1966.

Another hooked rendering of "Garden Orchard and Vine." Edana (Edith Dana) pattern / Quail Hill Designs. Slide processed May 1969.

Close-up of "Garden Orchard and Vine." Edana (Edith Dana) pattern / Quail Hill Designs. Slide processed May 1969.

"Hitchcock Center" was exhibited at the 1957 Women's International Exposition in New York City, New York. Pearl McGown pattern / Old Sturbridge Village / W. Cushing and Company.

New Hampshire rug hooking artist, teacher, and our photographer Hallie Hall appropriately displayed her hooked reproduction of a Peale still life on an artist's easel. Hooked in 1980. Slide processed September 1980.

"Basket of Goodies" offers a variety of fruit. Pearl McGown pattern / Old Sturbridge Village / W. Cushing and Company. Slide processed August 1972.

Less than optimum lighting did not stop viewers from enjoying this display of hooked fruit. Slide processed September 1980.

More of summer's bounty. Slide processed September 1980.

Lush tiers of fruit. From an old print. Identified by our photographer Hallie Hall as made by George Wells in 1957. Wells (1906–1988), designer and rug maker, maintained a studio in New York's Long Island district. His hooked rugs were and still are sought after by an impressive list of admirers. The George Wells Ruggery continues to operate in Glen Cove, New York, under the direction of Joseph Misiakiewicz.

A scalloped border of posies frames a basket crammed with fruits of the earth. Karlkraft pattern / Braid-Aid. Slide processed June 1960.

Off to a good start. "Ceres" features overflowing baskets and horns of plenty. Pearl McGown pattern / Old Sturbridge Village / W. Cushing and Company. Slide processed August 1973.

Opposite page:
"Ceres," a glorious hooked harvest, is symbolic of the good life. Pearl McGown pattern / Old Sturbridge Village / W. Cushing and Company. Slide processed August 1973.

A prize-winning "September Song." Grapes dominate and surround a fruited central motif. Pearl McGown pattern / Old Sturbridge Village / W. Cushing and Company. Slide processed November 1960.

Opposite page:
Close-up of another interpretation of "September Song." Pearl McGown pattern / Old Sturbridge Village / W. Cushing and Company. Slide processed October 1970.

Nothing but grapes. Close-up of "Santa Vittoria." Pearl McGown pattern / Old Sturbridge Village / W. Cushing and Company. Slide processed August 1969.

Opposite page:
"Morley's Choice" complements both garden and forest. Hooked by Evelyn Sober, Long Island, New York. Margaret Mackenzie–Skaket / Heirloom Rug pattern. Slide processed June 1959.

A smaller version of the aforementioned "Morley's Choice." Hooked by
Elsie Helm. Dated [19]59. Margaret Mackenzie–Skaket / Heirloom Rug
pattern. Slide processed August 1959.

"Morley's Choice" was a popular pattern to hook. Margaret Mackenzie–
Skaket / Heirloom Rug pattern. Slide processed July 1963.

Identified by our photographer Hallie Hall as "Fay's Fruit Rug." Slide processed September 1980.

Opposite page:
"Earth's Endowment"
was a good design on
which to learn how to
hook fifteen different
fruits. Pearl McGown
pattern / Old Sturbridge
Village / W. Cushing and
Company. Slide pro-
cessed September 1980.

In 1956, Alice Kelley hooked a handsome 8' x 10' "Harvest." Pearl McGown pattern / Old Sturbridge Village / W. Cushing and Company.

Opposite page:
A prize-winning "Country Fair." Pearl McGown pattern / Old Sturbridge Village / W. Cushing and Company. Slide processed November 1958.

Tullie Millard's 1956 "Harvest." Pearl McGown pattern / Old Sturbridge Village / W. Cushing and Company.

The outer border of this "Harvest" is yet to be hooked. Maker identified only as Elizabeth. Pearl McGown pattern / Old Sturbridge Village / W. Cushing and Company.

"Harvest" as it nears completion. Pearl McGown pattern / Old Sturbridge Village / W. Cushing and Company. Slide processed June 1972.

"Thanksgiving" celebrates a plentiful harvest. Hooked by Lilly Strange of Long Island, New York. Heirloom Rug pattern. Slide processed April 1958.

Half-round "Vegetable Medley" features seldom-hooked gifts from the garden. Joan Moshimer design–W. Cushing and Company. Slide processed September 1980.

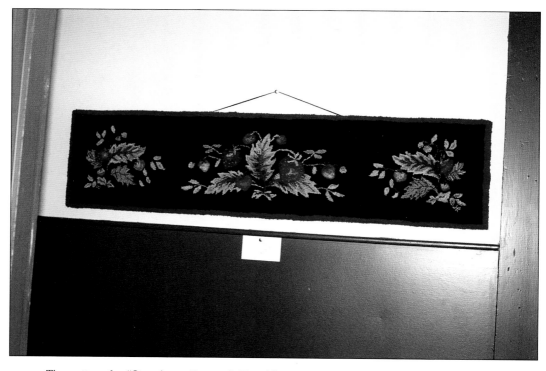

The pattern for "Strawberry Deacon's Bench" was fashioned into a hanging banner. Joan Moshimer design–W. Cushing and Company. Slide processed September 1980.

Opposite page:
Hooked fruit was quite versatile
both on and off the floor. Slide
processed September 1980.

Oriental Designs

Maine native Edward Sands Frost (1843–1894) is credited with being the first widely known commercial maker of hooked rug patterns. Frost's "Turkish" designs were reproduced by numerous pattern makers including, in the 1950s, Pearl McGown. "Frost Oriental No. 134." Pearl McGown pattern / Old Sturbridge Village / W. Cushing and Company and Charlotte Stratton / Greenfield Village–Henry Ford Museum / Maine State Museum.

Opposite page:
"Frost Oriental No. 134" completed. Pearl
McGown pattern / Old Sturbridge Village / W.
Cushing and Company and Charlotte
Stratton / Greenfield Village–Henry Ford
Museum / Maine State Museum.

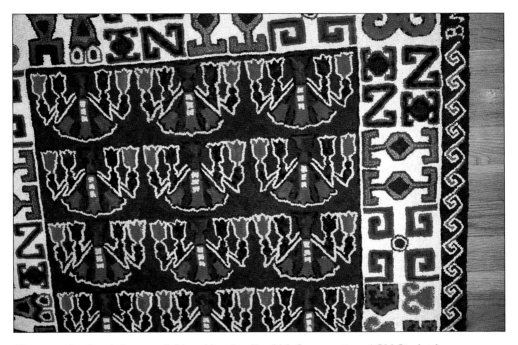

Close-up of a detailed center field and border. Pearl McGown pattern / Old Sturbridge Village / W. Cushing and Company. Slide processed October 1976.

Opposite page:
Close-up of "Nomad Runner."
Pearl McGown pattern / Old
Sturbridge Village / W. Cushing and
Company and Charlotte Stratton /
Greenfield Village–Henry Ford
Museum / Maine State Museum.

"Afshari." Predominant colors of gold, green, and deep red are highlighted by touches of white. Pearl McGown pattern / Old Sturbridge Village / W. Cushing and Company. Slide processed August 1971.

An eye-catching medallion draws your attention inward. Hooked by Kathy Pappas. Teacher Hallie Hall. Slide processed September 1980.

Hooked rug exhibits featured a wide variety of designs, including this lively Oriental. Slide processed September 1980.

The horizontal panels of "Peru" were inspired by ancient artifacts. Pearl McGown pattern / Old Sturbridge Village / W. Cushing and Company. Slide processed November 1958.

"Peru" in shades of green and gold. Pearl McGown pattern / Old Sturbridge Village / W. Cushing and Company. Slide processed February 1965.

Rich reds reign supreme. "Peru." Pearl McGown pattern / Old Sturbridge Village / W. Cushing and Company. Slide processed October 1967.

Another view of the aforementioned "Peru." Pearl McGown pattern / Old Sturbridge Village / W. Cushing and Company. Slide processed October 1967.

Side by side. The curving and flowing lines of a Persian design join angular motifs of an Oriental pattern. Slide processed September 1980.

A Persian beauty worthy of a prize-winning ribbon. Slide processed March 1961.

Fit for a Persian "Empress." Pearl McGown pattern / Old Sturbridge Village / W. Cushing and Company. Slide processed June 1964.

Another royal "Empress." Hooked by Anne Blouser. Pearl McGown
pattern / Old Sturbridge Village / W. Cushing and Company. Slide processed March 1966.

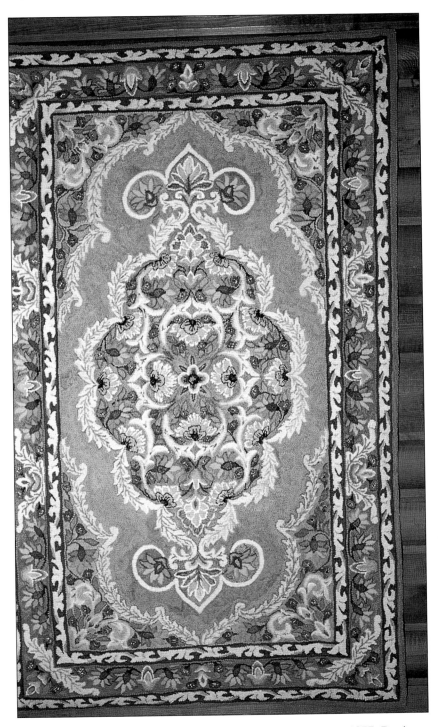

"Riza," a rug pattern of Iranian heritage. Hooked by Jane Lett in 1957. Pearl McGown pattern / Old Sturbridge Village / W. Cushing and Company.

Another lavish version of "Riza." Pearl McGown pattern / Old Sturbridge Village / W. Cushing and Company. Slide processed June 1960.

Hooked Orientals imitated knotted Orientals and were often mistaken for the genuine article. Slide processed February 1965.

"Persian Miniature." Hooked by Doris Perriea in 1957. Exhibited at the Silver Tray International. Location and date unknown. Pearl McGown pattern / Old Sturbridge Village / W. Cushing and Company.

Another rug hooker's version of "Persian Miniature." Slide processed April 1964. Pearl McGown pattern / Old Sturbridge Village / W. Cushing and Company.

Fluid lines and soft colors are characteristic of a "Kirman." Ruth Hall pattern / W. Cushing and Company. Slide processed July 1961.

Every bit of floor space at an exhibit was covered with hooked Orientals. Slide processed February 1966.

"Omar Khayyám" (44" x 68"), named for the ancient Persian poet and astronomer, was a challenging pattern to hook. Pearl McGown pattern / Old Sturbridge Village / W. Cushing and Company. Slide processed November 1959.

A larger "Omar Khayyám" (60" x 84"). Pearl McGown pattern / Old Sturbridge Village / W. Cushing and Company. Slide processed February 1978.

For a more authentic look, rug makers often added fringe to their hooked Orientals. "The Sheik." Pearl McGown pattern / Old Sturbridge Village / W. Cushing and Company. Slide processed August 1971.

A bold central medallion dominates. Slide processed June 1960.

Our photographer Hallie Hall made note that Ethel Johnson hooked this original
Oriental-style rug in 1955.

"Oriental #2 Ladik," a handsome hooked prayer rug complete with fringe. Joan Moshimer design–W. Cushing and Company. Slide processed September 1980.

In 1957, two variations of "Sacred Flame" were underway. Pearl McGown pattern / Old Sturbridge Village / W. Cushing and Company.

Opposite page:
Hooked Persian and
Oriental designs comple-
ment each other. Slide
processed June 1972.

"Peking." Rug hookers welcomed new venues to hone their craft. Pearl McGown pattern / Old Sturbridge Village / W. Cushing and Company. Slide processed August 1973.

"Ori-Dono," named for a silk museum Pearl McGown visited in Kyoto, Japan, invites you to look beyond its surface beauty and seek out hidden meanings. Information from Pearl McGown's 1966 book *The Lore and Lure of Hooked Rugs*. Pearl McGown pattern / Old Sturbridge Village / W. Cushing and Company. Slide processed September 1980.

"Lung Dragon," gold, green, and rising with the smoke. Pearl McGown pattern / Old Sturbridge Village / W. Cushing and Company. Slide processed August 1973.

Another "Lung Dragon." Pearl McGown pattern / Old Sturbridge Village / W. Cushing and Company. Slide processed August 1973.

"Lute Player." Joan Moshimer design–W. Cushing and Company. Slide processed
September 1980.

Opposite page:
Ornamental diamonds rest
within a lattice-work frame.
Hooked by Alice Kelley in
1957. Pearl McGown pattern /
Old Sturbridge Village / W.
Cushing and Company.

Geometric Designs

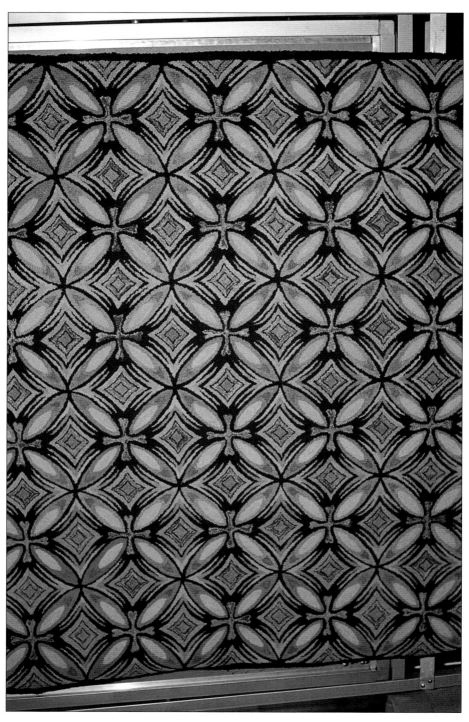

Complex repeat patterns were tedious work for any rug hooker. "Illusion." Pearl McGown pattern / Old Sturbridge Village / W. Cushing and Company. Slide processed October 1970.

A geometric design that creates an optical "Illusion." Pearl McGown pattern / Old Sturbridge Village / W. Cushing and Company. Slide processed April 1965.

"Vermont Geometric." Simple yet pleasing. Pearl McGown pattern / Old Sturbridge Village / W. Cushing and Company. Slide processed September 1980.

Opposite page:
Traditional quilt patterns were often used as hooked rug patterns. Slide processed October 1971.

The "Crossed Paddles" rug pattern was a great design for using up the odds and ends that every rug hooker accumulates. Heirloom Rug pattern. Slide processed September 1980.

An intriguing geometric design highlighted by eight stars. Slide processed March 1961.

A different approach to the aforementioned pattern. Slide processed July 1963.

Snowflake-like blocks are reminiscent of childhood paper cutouts. Slide processed August 1971.

"Lotus" is an abstract approach to its floral namesake. Pearl McGown pattern / Old
Sturbridge Village / W. Cushing and Company. Slide processed March 1962.

Right:
"Fountain of Youth" was inspired by Pearl McGown's trip
to Mexico, its famous sparkling waters, and a tile wall in
the Hotel Penafield. Information from Pearl McGown's
1966 book *The Lore and Lure of Hooked Rugs*. Identified
by Hallie Hall as "by Hick's student," perhaps the name
of a fellow rug hooking teacher. Pearl McGown pattern /
Old Sturbridge Village / W. Cushing and Company.

In Hallie Hall's own words, "This is the center of a very large lamb's tongue [rug]." Many hooked rug pattern makers offered the popular lamb's tongue or clamshell designs in a variety of sizes. Slide processed August 1960.

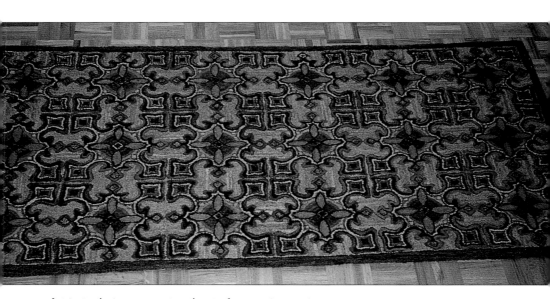

Intricate designs come together to form an impressive repeat pattern.

Butter Mold Patterns
and Quilt Traditions

In each block a "Provincial" pattern. Hooked by Gwen Peters. Initialed GMP. Dated 1976. Heirloom Rug pattern. Slide processed September 1980.

"Butter Molds" calls to mind bygone days and lost traditions. Hooked by Alice Kelley. Margaret Mackenzie–Skaket / Heirloom Rug pattern.

More "Butter Molds." Initialed SRS. Dated 1979. Margaret Mackenzie–Skaket / Heirloom Rug pattern. Slide processed September 1980.

Rugs were often hooked to commemorate weddings and anniversaries. Note the well-dressed couple under the fanciful floral sprays. Bearing two sets of initials. Dated 1921. Slide processed June 1959.

Opposite page:
Quilt designs influenced rug hookers and pattern makers. Dated 1960. Slide processed June 1960.

Recalling traditional quilt motifs. Initialed GPB and ALB. Dated 1953 and 1960. Slide processed March 1961.

Inspired by appliquéd quilts. Simplistic cutout designs placed against a neutral background. Slide processed February 1980.

Cultural traditions of the Pennsylvania Dutch were appealing to rug hookers. "Pennsylvania Dutch Hexes." Pearl McGown pattern / Old Sturbridge Village / W. Cushing and Company. Slide processed September 1980.

Opposite page:
A whimsical caricature of "The Happy Hooker—Hallie Hall" rests among a set of Anita Allen–designed hooked chair pads and an "All Butter Mold" rug. W. Cushing and Company patterns. Slide processed September 1980.

Childhood Themes

"The Lambs" frolic on grassy hills ripe with strawberries. Margaret Mackenzie–Skaket / Heirloom Rug pattern. Slide processed November 1958.

Right:
Another version of "Merry-Go-Round." Pearl McGown pattern / Old Sturbridge Village / W. Cushing and Company. June 1960.

"Merry-Go-Round," hooked by Mary Ramsay of Hauppauge, Long Island, New York. Teacher Hallie Hall. Appeared in Pearl McGown's 1966 book *The Lore and Lure of Hooked Rugs*. Initialed MR. Dated 1962. Pearl McGown pattern / Old Sturbridge Village / W. Cushing and Company. Slide processed July 1963.

A rug to delight any child. A bowl of honey (or is it hot porridge?) attracts both "Baby Bear" and bees. Hooked by Betty Champlain. Margaret Mackenzie–Skaket / Heirloom Rug pattern. Slide processed September 1961.

"Honey Bear" out for a stroll. Pearl McGown pattern / Old Sturbridge Village / W. Cushing and Company. Slide processed December 1972.

Hooked portrait of a "Happy Clown." Pearl McGown pattern / Old Sturbridge Village / W. Cushing and Company.

A smiling little fellow bearing the name Olga. "Patches the Clown." Joan Moshimer design–W. Cushing and Company.

"Patches the Clown" and his twin brother. Joan Moshimer design–W. Cushing and Company. Slide processed June 1972.

The four seasons of the "Sun Bonnet Sisters." Hooked by Gladys Fountain. Slide processed September 1961.

"Sun Bonnet Girls" undertaking daily chores. Slide processed June 1973.

A hooked interpretation of a child's drawing rests beside the aforementioned "Sun Bonnet Girls." Slide processed September 1980.

"Little Boy Blue" recalls a favorite childhood nursery rhyme. Heirloom Rug pattern. Slide processed November 1958.

"Little Red Riding Hood" receives a hug after an encounter with the big, bad wolf. Slide processed February 1980.

Beloved characters from the Walt Disney animated movie *Bambi* were copied, hooked, and used to upholster a chair seat. Some rug hookers, unaware of copyright laws, innocently reproduced images for their own enjoyment. Today copyright laws are more strictly enforced and ethical rug makers will not reproduce another artist's work without permission. Slide processed October 1980.

Opposite page:
Animal figures from the
Beatrix Potter storybooks
form a panel hooked by Jo
Meirsmer. Slide processed
February 1980.

"The Three Men in a Tub." Ruth Hall pattern / W. Cushing and Company. Slide processed June 1960.

Dancing a jig. Two gentlemanly mice, one clad in a kilt, accompany a plucky lady mouse. From the original Claretta Higgins keepsake nursery rug bearing the date 1953 and used as wall décor in the Crawford Hollidge's Wellesley, Massachusetts, store. As illustrated in Stella Hay Rex's 1953 book, *Choice Hooked Rugs*. Slide processed June 1973.

Fashioned after a "Krazy Quilt." Childhood memories were hooked and preserved for Greg. Dated 1958. Margaret Mackenzie–Skaket / Heirloom Rug pattern. Slide processed February 1959.

A red-letter alphabet mingles with all creatures great and small. Our photographer Hallie Hall identifies this design as being original. Slide processed December 1963.

Chronicling the lives of fanciful forest folk, *Gnomes,* written by Wil Huygen, illustrated by Rien Poortvliet, and published in 1976, was popular with both children, adults, and some rug hookers. A panel of hooked "Gnomes" is appropriately displayed among the hooked mushrooms. Slide processed September 1980.

Native American

North American West Coast Indian tribes carved symbolic figures on their totem poles. Rug makers re-created these images on hooked panels. Hallie Hall's totem appears on the right. Pearl McGown pattern / Old Sturbridge Village / W. Cushing and Company. Slide processed August 1971.

Close-up of the aforementioned hooked totems.

Portrait of an "Indian Chief" rests upon "Santa Fe." Pearl McGown patterns / Old Sturbridge Village / W. Cushing and Company. Slide processed September 1980.

Christmas Joy

Santa Claus, a hooked portrait. Slide processed June 1973.

"Bringing In the Yule Log." Framed in ribbon, holly, and pine and sporting a prize-winning ribbon. Margaret Hunt Masters design / Prairie Craft House. Slide processed November 1958.

Another prize winner. "Bringing In the Yule Log." Margaret Hunt Masters design / Prairie Craft House. Slide processed November 1960.

A pipe organ forms the backdrop for "Choir Boys." Note the ornate hooked frame.
Margaret Hunt Masters design / Prairie Craft House. Slide processed November 1960.

Charles Dickens would be pleased with this hooked vignette of Tiny Tim's home and family. "Crachit Family." Margaret Hunt Masters design / Prairie Craft House. Slide processed November 1960.

"Silent Night." The village church on Christmas Eve. Margaret Hunt Masters design / Prairie Craft House. Slide processed November 1960.

More hooked holiday treasures. "Merry Christmas." Edana (Edith Dana) pattern / Quail Hill Designs. Slide processed September 1980.

Opposite page:
Hooked "Merry Christmas" greetings come in all forms: stockings, banner, and rug. Edana (Edith Dana) pattern / Quail Hill Designs. Slide processed February 1965.

The "Holy Family" portrayed against a stained-glass sky. Joan Moshimer design–W. Cushing and Company. Slide processed September 1980.

Religious Themes

A portrait of Jesus holding a lamb. Hooked by Hallie Hall. Exhibited at the 1954 Women's International Exposition, New York City, New York.

"The Last Supper—Christ and the Disciples." Hooked by Edna Fleming. Displayed at a church in Maine. Slide processed June 1972.

Butterflies and Bees

An original study complete with the iridescent qualities of a butterfly's wings.

Bright, beautiful, and taking on the shape of the butterfly it portrays. Identified by our photographer Hallie Hall as being an original design.

Butterfly chair pad among the hooked flowers. Slide processed September 1980.

"Butterflies." Hooked by Lilly Strange of Long Island, New York. Teacher Hallie Hall. Karlkraft pattern / Braid-Aid. Slide processed July 1963.

Another version of "Butterflies," with a sky blue background. Initialed FL. Dated 1977. Karlkraft pattern / Braid-Aid. Slide processed September 1980.

More delightful "Summer Butterflies." Joan Moshimer design–W. Cushing and Company. Slide processed September 1980.

Opposite page:
"Silken Wings." Pearl McGown
pattern / Old Sturbridge Village /
W. Cushing and Company. Slide
processed October 1967.

"Bright Wings" underway. Pearl McGown pattern / Old Sturbridge Village / W. Cushing and Company. Slide processed September 1965.

Close-up of bees on sprigs of clover.

Birds

"Chanticleer," identified by Hallie Hall as an original design, was incorrectly labeled "Chanticlear." Exhibited at the 1957 Women's International Exposition in New York City, New York.

Right:
Twin roosters with
fine plumage.
Hooked in 1957.

Opponents face off. "Rooster and Cat." Exhibited at the 1957 Women's International Exposition in New York City, New York. Pearl McGown pattern / Old Sturbridge Village / W. Cushing and Company.

Prize-winning rooster poised on a rock. Slide processed November 1958.

Atop a chicken-coop roof and signaling the break of day. "Rooster," also known as "Christmas Morn." Pearl McGown pattern / Old Sturbridge Village / W. Cushing and Company. Slide processed June 1961.

"Rooster," another version. Pearl McGown pattern / Old Sturbridge Village / W. Cushing and Company.

Always looking for food. "Farmyard Geese." Initialed PW. Dated [19]72. Joan Moshimer design–W. Cushing and Company. Slide processed June 1973.

Betty (Elizabeth) Maley's "Farmyard Geese." Joan Moshimer design–W. Cushing and Company (also known as Craftsman Studio). Slide processed September 1980.

Opposite page:
"Bird Bell Pull." Pearl McGown
pattern / Old Sturbridge Village / W.
Cushing and Company. Slide
processed August 1971.

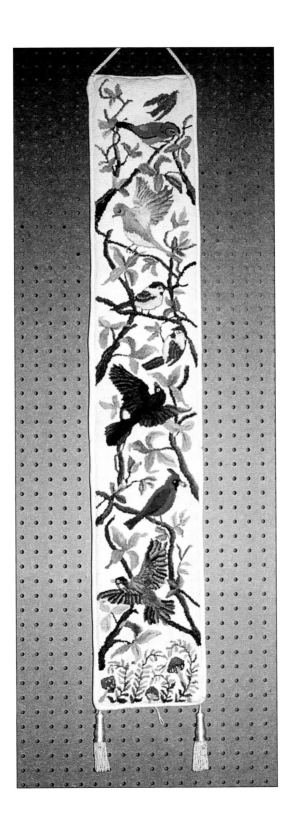

"Bird Watch Oval," an ornithologist's dream. Hooked by Elsie Young. Teacher Hallie
Hall. Edana (Edith Dana) pattern / Quail Hill Designs. Slide processed July 1963.

In 1957, Margaret Brown hooked a likeness of the Currier and Ives print "The Happy Family." Pearl McGown pattern / Old Sturbridge Village / W. Cushing and Company and Heirloom Rug pattern.

"Wedding Plate." Pearl McGown pattern / Old Sturbridge Village / W. Cushing and Company. Slide processed June 1973.

A pillow top "Road Runner." Joan Moshimer design–W. Cushing and Company. Slide processed August 1972.

Tote bag adorned with two feathered friends joins a "Partridge in a Pear Tree." Pearl McGown pattern / Old Sturbridge Village / W. Cushing and Company. Slide processed September 1980.

"Lonely" owl, wide-eyed, watching, and mounted on old board. Pearl McGown pattern / Old Sturbridge Village / W. Cushing and Company. Slide processed February 1980.

"Lonely" owl set against a glowing full moon. Pearl McGown pattern / Old Sturbridge Village / W. Cushing and Company. Slide processed August 1973.

A "Pheasant" in flight keeps "Lonely" owl company. Pearl McGown patterns / Old Sturbridge Village / W. Cushing and Company.

"Great Horned Owl" mounted on a wooden board. Joan Moshimer design–W. Cushing and Company. Slide processed August 1970.

Captured in an oval frame. "Great Horned Owl." Joan Moshimer design–W. Cushing and Company. Slide processed April 1971.

"Great Horned Owl" framed. Joan Moshimer design–W. Cushing and Company.

An owl family gathering. Slide processed October 1969.

Whimsical owls of a feather flock together. Slide processed September 1984.

Opposite page:
"Wood Ducks"
encounter a determined
turtle. Edana (Edith
Dana) pattern / Quail
Hill Designs. Slide
processed June 1960.

"On the Wing." Initialed UAC. Dated [19]78. Pearl McGown pattern / Old Sturbridge Village / W. Cushing and Company. Slide processed September 1980.

Opposite page:
"Canadian Snow Geese." Initialed JR. Dated [19]84. Jane McGown Flynn pattern / The House of Price, Inc.–Charco Patterns. Slide processed July 1986.

Highlighted by a full moon. Another interpretation of "On the Wing." Pearl McGown pattern / Old Sturbridge Village / W. Cushing and Company. Slide processed September 1980.

Opposite page:
Oceanside treasures including a framed "Young Stilt." Joan Moshimer design–W. Cushing and Company. Slide processed September 1980.

A hooked snapshot of seabirds is boldly framed by fanciful flowers and foliage. Identified by our photographer Hallie Hall as an original design. Slide processed November 1958.

Feathered friends like none found in nature. Slide processed November 1981.

An exotic fowl with an impressive crest. Slide processed November 1970.

Patriotic Eagles

A patriotic and stately eagle. Hooked in 1958 by Ruth Haseney of Long Island, New York. As noted by our photographer Hallie Hall, "Women from New Hampshire crafted an 8' x 10' rug of similar pattern for the home of President Eisenhower."

"His Majesty" displaying an impressive wingspan. Pearl McGown pattern / Old Sturbridge Village / W. Cushing and Company. Slide processed June 1960.

Hooked in shades of blue and gold. "His Majesty." Pearl McGown pattern / Old Sturbridge Village / W. Cushing and Company. Slide processed March 1961.

Bronze scrolls, lush and elaborate, frame "His Majesty." Hooked by Hallie Hall. Pearl McGown pattern / Old Sturbridge Village / W. Cushing and Company. Slide processed 1961.

Yet another hooked rendering of "His Majesty." Pearl McGown pattern / Old Sturbridge Village / W. Cushing and Company. Slide processed June 1972.

A regal "Wendall Eagle." Ralph Burnham / Ruth Hall design / W. Cushing and Company. Slide processed September 1980.

Stars representing the original thirteen colonies surround this stately "Clemson Eagle."
Karlkraft pattern / Braid-Aid. Slide processed October 1970.

Stars and stripes compose the body of an eagle tightly grasping an olive branch, arrows, and ribbon bearing the Latin phrase "E Pluribus Unum"—one out of many. Slide processed April 1955.

A frame of oak leaves, ribbons, and corner stars complement a patriotic eagle. Identified by Hallie Hall as "Joe's Class." Karlkraft pattern / Braid-Aid. Slide processed October 1961.

The aforementioned pattern hooked with a different color scheme.

A hooked tribute to the "Great Seal of the United States." Slide processed October 1961.

A half-round "Eagle" against a sky blue background. Edana (Edith Dana) pattern / Quail Hill Designs. Slide processed June 1964.

"Vermont Union Rug" was adapted from a popular Edward Sands Frost (1843–1894) pattern. Helen Prouty Tracy of Vermont began hooking the rug in 1941 under the tutelage of rug hooking teacher and designer Charlotte Stratton, set the project aside for many years, and completed the work in 1981 under the direction of rug hooking teacher Anne Ashworth. Information from *Rug Hooker News and Views*, Issue 54, Volume 9, Number 6, September-October 1981. Slide processed November 1981.

"Frost Eagle." Initialed SRM. Dated 1958. Edana (Edith Dana) pattern /
Quail Hill Designs.

"1820 Eagle," complete with shamrocks, thistles, rose, and buds. Hooked by Rose Puglisi. Karlkraft pattern / Braid-Aid. Slide processed November 1962.

An unadorned eagle perched on a bench and surrounded by hooked flowers. Slide processed September 1980.

All Creatures Great and Small

Peace and serenity can be found at "The Pool." Edana (Edith Dana) pattern / Quail Hill Designs.

Ready to dart. Tiny "Chipmunk" on a stump. Initialed P.J. New Earth Designs. Slide
processed May 1973.

A prize-winning "Chatterbox." Heirloom Rug pattern. Slide processed November 1960.

Masked "Little Bandit." Pearl McGown pattern / Old Sturbridge Village / W. Cushing and Company. Slide processed February 1980.

A "Kitty" named Oliver. Lib Callaway Patterns / Margaret Siano–Hook Nook. Slide processed February 1980.

Minnie Thing of Maine hooked her first rug, "Pussy Cat Welcome," in 1957. Frost pattern / W. Cushing and Company and Charlotte Stratton / Greenfield Village–Henry Ford Museum / Maine State Museum.

A collage of cats set against shards of blue. Slide processed June 1960.

Hallie Hall identified "Cats and Dogs" as an original design. Slide processed March 1966.

"Deer in the Woodland." Ralph Burnham pattern / Ruth Hall / W. Cushing and Company. Slide processed January 1970.

"Woodland Family." Mother deer and fawn. Anita Allen design / W. Cushing and Company. Slide processed September 1980.

Opposite page:
Inspired by a photograph, Massachusetts rug hooking artist and teacher Annie Spring was awarded first prize at the 1960 Women's International Exposition in New York City, New York, for her hooked composition of a feeding deer. Slide processed November 1960.

Time for a drink. Deer at waters edge. Slide processed September 1980.

Contented New Hampshire bovine. "Sweet William." Designed by Heather Erskine and hooked by Ann Winterling. Slide processed February 1980.

Prize-winning hooked portrait of a beloved horse. Slide processed November 1958.

"The Prize." Stable gear frames an equine duo. Initialed GEJ. Dated [19]60. Slide processed June 1960.

"Old New England Coach Line" depicts a horse-drawn carriage filled with passengers. Ralph Burnham pattern / Ruth Hall / W. Cushing and Company. Slide processed February 1965.

"Patriot" Paul Revere, upon his trusty steed, warns of the British invasion. Note the initials LIB on the stern of the moored vessel. Lib Callaway Patterns / Margaret Siano–Hook Nook. Slide processed November 1981.

"Fairfield Huntsman." In the original pattern, the figure on the right holds a raised gun. Most likely hooked during the Vietnam War era, this nonviolent rug maker chose to eliminate the firearm. Ralph Burnham pattern / Ruth Hall / W. Cushing and Company. Slide processed October 1969.

An armed "Fairfield Huntsman." Ralph Burnham pattern / Ruth Hall / W. Cushing and Company. Slide processed September 1980.

Pictorials—Rural Life

"The Way It Was" in simpler times. Edana (Edith Dana) pattern / Quail Hill Designs.
Slide processed September 1984.

Village scene with carriages and train. "Early Railroad Days." Ralph Burnham pattern / Ruth Hall / W. Cushing and Company. Slide processed September 1980.

"T'is and T'aint"; a look at country life. Pearl McGown pattern / Old Sturbridge Village / W. Cushing and Company. Slide processed September 1980.

Close-up of "T'is and T'aint." Pearl McGown pattern / Old Sturbridge Village / W. Cushing and Company. Slide processed February 1980.

Autumn days in a New England town. Hooked by Dorothy McNabb. Identified by Hallie Hall as an original design. Slide processed July 1963.

Hooked church still in the making.

A nearly completed "Castle in Spain." Hooked by Ann Winterling of New Hampshire. Adapted from an Heirloom Rug pattern.

Opposite page:
"Little Log Cabin" and
"Brandenburg (Havel)"
seal. Slide processed
September 1980.

LITTLE LOG
CABIN
Designer
Hooked by Jean Geiger
Whitfield, N.H.
Teacher: Hallie Hall

BRANDENBURG HAVEL SEAL
Designer: Hallie Hall
Hooked by: Fay Leichter
East Washington
Teacher: Hallie Hall

"Little House." Hooked by Mary Jane Robinson. Slide processed September 1980.

Another version of "Little House." Slide processed June 1972.

"Antique Shop." Filled to capacity and awaiting customers.

Opposite page:
A partial view of a
half-round "Lighted
Windows Welcome."
Heirloom Rug
pattern.

The highest bid takes the lot at the "Country Auction." Edana (Edith Dana) pattern /
Quail Hill Designs. Slide processed September 1980.

A street scene of yesteryear. "The Liar's Bench." Karlkraft pattern / Braid-Aid. Slide processed June 1960.

Another version of "The Liar's Bench." Hooked in 1961. Karlkraft pattern / Braid-Aid. Slide processed September 1961.

Yet another "The Liar's Bench." Karlkraft pattern / Braid-Aid. Slide processed 1980.

An interior view of the "Country Store." Hooked by Jo Parker. Karlkraft pattern / Braid-Aid. Slide processed October 1961.

Covered Bridges
and Woodlands

"Covered Bridge" over icy waters. Karlkraft pattern / Braid-Aid.

At play beside the "Old Covered Bridge." Adapted from a nostalgic painting of bygone days. Heirloom Rug pattern. Slide processed April 1964.

A ruralist's dream. "Old Covered Bridge" and a "Snug Haven." Heirloom Rug pattern. Pearl McGown pattern / Old Sturbridge Village / W. Cushing and Company. Slide processed June 1972.

Autumn leaves fall on an "Old Covered Bridge." Heirloom Rug pattern. Slide processed February 1980.

The "Old Covered Bridge" was popular with rug hookers, was admired by many, and traveled from exhibit to exhibit. Heirloom Rug pattern. Slide processed September 1980.

"Sturbridge Covered Bridge" set against the reds and golds of autumn in New England. Hooked by Hallie Hall. Pearl McGown pattern / Old Sturbridge Village / W. Cushing and Company. Slide processed February 1977.

A new beginning. "Covered Bridge" in spring. Karlkraft pattern / Braid-Aid. Slide processed February 1960.

The golden glow of aged wood is reflected in still waters. "Covered Bridge." Slide processed September 1980.

A trio of puffy clouds floats above a gristmill. Slide processed September 1980.

A view of the lake through "The Birches." Note the hooked gray frame. Hooked by Hallie Hall in 1959. Pearl McGown pattern / Old Sturbridge Village / W. Cushing and Company. Slide processed August 1959.

Winter Scenes

What could be more fun than snow "Skiing"? Initialed AJK. Dated [19]67. Edana (Edith Dana) pattern / Quail Hill Designs. Slide processed June 1967.

There was frost in the air at this hooked rug exhibit. Winter scenes galore. Slide processed September 1980.

"Liza," coming in from the fields, hangs above the "Holy Family" and two versions of "Christmas in the Valley." With limited space at rug exhibits, unlikely groupings often took place. Eclectic but delightful. The "Liza" pattern, hooked by Hallie Hall, was incorrectly labeled "Lisa." "Liza" is a Jane McGown Flynn pattern / The House of Price, Inc.–Charco Patterns. The three round scenes are Joan Moshimer designs–W. Cushing and Company. Slide processed February 1980.

Delicate beauty. A close-up of "Snowflakes." Hooked by Ruth Durelman in 1957. Pearl McGown pattern / Old Sturbridge Village / W. Cushing and Company.

No two "Snowflakes" are alike, even if they were hooked from the same pattern. Pearl McGown pattern / Old Sturbridge Village / W. Cushing and Company. Slide processed March 1962.

A Nostalgic Look
Back at Transportation

Days of the horseless carriage. "Antique Car." Pearl McGown pattern / Old Sturbridge Village / W. Cushing and Company. Slide processed August 1969.

The street lamp is lit as evening approaches, and moonlight pours through the back window of this "Antique Car." Pearl McGown pattern / Old Sturbridge Village / W. Cushing and Company. Slide processed June 1973.

Another "Antique Car" on the road. Initialed LEB. Dated 1968. Pearl McGown pattern / Old Sturbridge Village / W. Cushing and Company. Slide processed November 1973.

A horse-drawn sleigh awaits passengers at a wintry Walton train station. Hooked by Liz Tompkins. Heirloom Rug pattern. Slide processed June 1973.

The early days of the "Baltimore and Ohio." Edana (Edith Dana) pattern / Quail Hill Designs. Slide processed June 1960.

Nautical Themes

Off the coast of Maine. "Portland Head Light." Pearl McGown pattern / Old Sturbridge Village / W. Cushing and Company.

Under full sail. "Clipper." Hooked in 1958. Heirloom Rug pattern.

"Mayflower II," a hooked replica of the ship that carried the Pilgrims to the New World. Pearl McGown pattern / Old Sturbridge Village / W. Cushing and Company. Slide processed October 1957.

Signs of the "Zodiac" encircle an ancient seagoing vessel. Heirloom Rug pattern. Slide processed October 1985.

"Weather Vanes," some of a nautical nature. Hooked by Anne Ashworth of Vermont. Teacher Hallie Hall. DiFranza Design. Slide processed June 1974.

Hooked Reproductions— Mimicking the Masters

Currier and Ives prints, popular in the nineteenth century, were also popular with twentieth-century rug hookers. "Frozen Up." Hooked by Hallie Hall in 1955. From the Currier and Ives print of the same name. Karlkraft pattern / Braid-Aid.

More of winter's icy blast. "Frozen Up." From the Currier and Ives print of the same name. Karlkraft pattern / Braid-Aid. Slide processed September 1980.

"Mr. & Mrs. Currier" bundled up and enjoying a sleigh ride. From the Currier and Ives print "The Road—Winter." Hooked by Hattie Pettit. Heirloom Rug pattern. Slide processed October 1961.

"Mr. & Mrs. Currier"
dashing through the snow.
From the Currier and Ives
print "The Road—Winter."
Hooked by Sarah Richards.
Heirloom Rug pattern. Slide
processed February 1980.

Close-up of the aforementioned "Mr. & Mrs. Currier." From the Currier and Ives print "The Road—Winter." Heirloom Rug pattern. Slide processed October 1980.

Pine boughs with sparse needles frame an oval vignette of "Mr. & Mrs. Currier" in their sleigh. From the Currier and Ives print "The Road—Winter." Edana (Edith Dana) pattern / Quail Hill Designs. Slide processed October 1961.

A rug any train enthusiast would love. "American Express Train." Hooked by Rose Puglisi. From one of the two Currier and Ives prints titled "Express Train." Heirloom Rug pattern. Slide processed February 1960.

Another "American Express Train" coming down the line. Hooked by Erlene Shaw of New Hampshire. Dated [19]76. From one of the two Currier and Ives prints titled "Express Train." Heirloom Rug pattern. Slide processed September 1980.

Pulling into the station and making another "Whistle Stop." Adapted from a painting recalling travel days of yesteryear. Heirloom Rug pattern. Slide processed April 1971.

One more "Whistle Stop." Heirloom Rug pattern. Slide processed June 1974.

Stoked up and ready to go after making a countryside "Whistle Stop." Hooked by Grace Kimball of New Hampshire. Heirloom Rug pattern. Slide processed February 1980.

A winter wonderland for "The Skaters." Hooked by Ann Winterling of New Hampshire.
Teacher Hallie Hall. Karlkraft pattern / Braid-Aid. Slide processed October 1980.

"Horse and Buggy Days," reproduced from a painting, recalls an era of summer days and blacksmith shops. Heirloom Rug pattern. Slide processed March 1961.

"Tiffany," a hooked reproduction of the original Tiffany "Iris and Magnolias" stained-glass panel. Jane McGown Flynn pattern / The House of Price, Inc.–Charco Patterns. Slide processed September 1984.

Imitating an Alexander Calder mobile. Initialed PHV. Dated [19]58.

Past images of elegant fashion. "Godey Ladies." Charlotte Stratton pattern / Ruth Davis / Yankee Peddler. Slide processed September 1980.

A switch in colors and a costume change for the "Godey Ladies." Charlotte Stratton pattern / Ruth Davis / Yankee Peddler. Slide processed September 1980.

Small Hooked Pieces

Visitors gather to admire wall hangings, bell pulls, framed pieces, table mats, chair pads, and pillows; all hooked and on display. Slide processed August 1970.

Opposite page:
More hooked art.
Slide processed
August 1970.

Small projects were always popular with rug hookers. Colorful pillows and chair pads added a note of cheer to any décor. Slide processed September 1980.

Exhibits always offered a variety of small hooked pieces. Slide processed September 1980.

Hooked dolls and more. Slide processed September 1980.

Small studies such as this paisley tile were often used as training aids for those wanting to become certified McGown rug hooking teachers. Pearl McGown design / Old Sturbridge Village / W. Cushing and Company. Slide processed May 1973.

Thank you, Hallie Hall (1908–2001), artist, teacher, and friend, for sharing your love and enthusiasm for hooked rugs, for touching so many lives, and for having the insight to document such a pivotal time in the rug hooking world—1950 through the mid-1980s.